Gifts of Spirit

Written & Illustrated by
Kimberly Heil

*A*nimals have always been an important part of my life and work as an artist. As an intuitive painter, I've always observed and researched animals. They emerge on my canvas without much prompting. From color to attitude, I am guided to bring them more fully into being. Telling the story about their gifts is what I like to share.

How to use this book

This is an interactive book intended to be used for:

- Animal identification
- Exploration of the natural gifts of animals
- Starting conversations about deeper personal values.
- Promoting quality time with your loved ones.
- Gaining deeper insight into your own personal values.
- Sparking creative thinking, listening, and learning.

Many cultures around the world believe that each animal has a spirit. The animal's spirit has its own unique set of qualities and gifts to share. These gifts offer us support, teaching, and guidance as we walk our life's journey. In this way, animals become our guides and teachers.

Additional Prompts

- Explore each animal's natural gifts by sharing your own personal experiences with each gift.
- Discuss the ways you identify with the animals in this book.
- Explore the animals with which you find it difficult to identify.
- What is your favorite animal?
- What are your personal gifts?
- Pick an animal whose gifts you would like to know more about. Research that animal and create your own drawing and page for this book.

Roadrunner

I am Randy the Roadrunner. I am a superfast runner. I like to keep my feet firmly on the ground. My moves are quick, sharp, and exact. I listen to my body when I need to rest.

Quick-thinking and accuracy
are my gifts.

What about you?

● Discuss an experience or situation when quick-thinking was important.

● What does accuracy mean to you?

Lynx

I am Leonora the Lynx. I love to run, jump, and play like all cats do. Nighttime is my playground. I love to find moments of quiet time.

Being graceful and playful are my gifts.

What about you?
- How are you graceful?
- When was the last time you played?

Giraffe

I am Gerry the Giraffe. I love being tall! My neck stretches long and high. It makes it easy to gather food in the trees. I can see all around the land from up here. I can see what others cannot.

Seeing from up high and reaching for the stars are my gifts.

What about you?

● Discuss your view from where you are standing and compare it to when you climb a hill.

● What do you want to do this year that is really important to you?

Elephant

I am Ebo the Elephant. I am gentle and very smart. My family and friends are always close. Nothing gets in my way. I can understand without hearing words.

Compassion and communicating without words are my gifts.

What about you?
- Describe a time when you experienced compassion.
- When were you able to understand someone without talking?

Owl

I am Otis the Owl. I love the stars, moon, and sounds of crickets at night. I can sit in my tree for a long time. I watch everything. My eyesight and hearing are very good. I fly silently through the air.

Patience and deep listening are my gifts.

What about you?
- When have you experienced patience?
- What does listening mean to you?

Rabbit

I am Ruthie the Rabbit. I am fast and clever. I always know what is going on around me. My family is very big. My soft fur keeps me warm.

Comfort and abundance are my gifts.

What about you?
- What brings you comfort?
- Describe abundance in your life.

Bee

I am Bella the Bee. I am always buzzing around. My hive is very important to me. It takes many of us to do all of the things that need to get done. We can do anything together.

Getting along and getting things done are my gifts.

What about you?

- Tell about a time when you got along with your friends.
- In what ways do you get things done?

Raccoon

I am Rocky the Raccoon. I am clever and creative. My mask is like a superhero's. Sometimes I get in trouble. I am curious and playful at night.

Adventure and problem-solving are my gifts.

What about you?

- What kind of adventure would you like to have?
- Describe a time when you had to solve a problem.

Tiger

I am Tal the Tiger. I am strong and fearless. My roar says how I am feeling. No two tigers' stripes are the same. I am brave when I protect my home.

Courage and being unique are my gifts.

What about you?
- Describe a time when you were brave.
- What is your favorite thing about being you?

Spider

I am Sam the Spider. I am a weaver. My web designs are the same on each side. I spin with delicate threads. I am patient in both creating and waiting.

Balance and creativity are my gifts.

What about you?
- Like a spider balancing on a web, what things do you balance in your life?
- In what ways are you creative?

Butterfly

I am Bailey the Butterfly. I go through many changes. I enter a cocoon crawling. I come out with wings. I love to explore new places.

Change and travel are my gifts.

What about you?
- In what ways have you grown or changed?
- Describe a place to which you would love to travel.

Dog

I am Dakota the Dog. I am always happy to see you. I love learning new tricks, protecting my home, and following you wherever you go.

Unconditional love and loyalty are my gifts.

What about you?
- What does unconditional love mean?
- Describe a time when you were loyal to someone.

Wolf

I am Wyatt the Wolf. I love to run with my pack. My friends and I watch out for each other. Together we protect the community we share. We are boundary keepers.

Intelligence and intuition are my gifts.

What about you?

- What does intelligence mean to you?
- Can you describe a time when you felt your intuition?

Crow

I am Crowley the Crow. I am very smart. I talk and tell stories with caw sounds. I use my voice to warn my friends when danger is near. Each time I try something new, I learn.

Honoring voice and storytelling are my gifts.

What about you?
- Describe a time when you had to use your voice to be brave.
- Tell a story all about yourself.

For my grandparents

Eileen and Michael

Caroline and Richard

for all your love, support, wisdom, grace, and laughter

Written and illustrated by Kimberly Heil
Designed by Heather Dakota

ISBN: 978-1-517-20834-9

10 9 8 7 6 5 4 3 2 1

Heather Dakota and associated logos are trademarks of Heather Dakota, LLC.
www.heatherdakota.com

Kimberly Heil is an artist, art therapist, and a reiki master. Her passion for art therapy helps others find healing through rediscovering their creativity and authentic voice. She explores art through the use of bright, bold colors, layers of texture, and her intuitive guidance.

Kim is enchanted by nature and her love of travel. She is a creative alchemist blending art and healing, a warrior for sacred expression, and a space holder for deep personal work. Deeply rooted in her ancestral lineage, Kim honors Mother Earth, (her resources and the gifts of the animals).

www.kimberlyheil.com

34066627R00020

Made in the USA
Columbia, SC
16 November 2018